# 50 GEM Lancashire

To Claire

with best wishes

Robert

ROBERT NICHOLLS

AMBERLEY

First published 2019

Amberley Publishing
The Hill, Stroud
Gloucestershire, GL5 4EP

www.amberley-books.com

British Library Cataloguing in Publication Data.
A catalogue record for this book is available from the British Library.

ISBN 978 1 4456 8493 2 (paperback)
ISBN 978 1 4456 8494 9 (ebook)

Origination by Amberley Publishing.

Printed in Great Britain.

# Contents

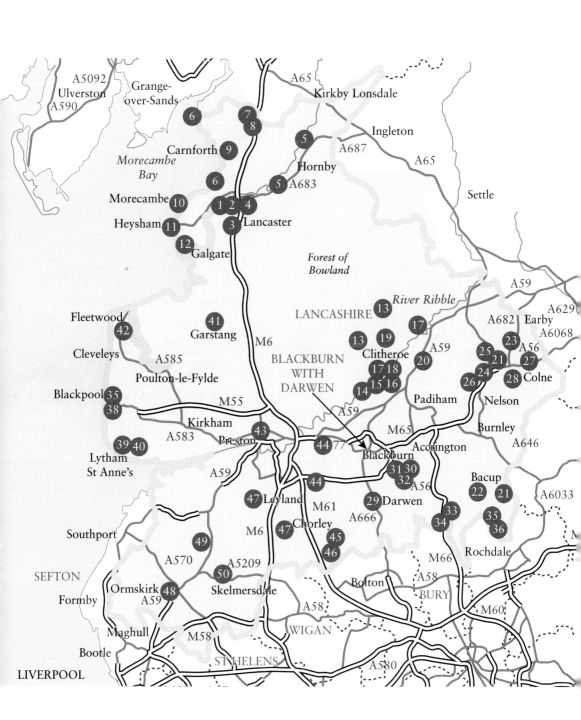

# Introduction

The word 'Lancashire' conjures up, for many, images of cotton mills and other forms of nineteenth-century industry, together with rows of terraced housing, industrial pollution and social deprivation. The reality could hardly be more different. Not only is the popular image outdated by all the changes of the modern world, it never was a completely true picture of the county.

Lancashire has many areas of great beauty, and is a fascinating county full of rich history, playing a large part in the history of England. It is no accident that the Queen is the Duke of Lancaster and that Lancashire is afforded 'Palatine' status.

Present-day Lancashire divides itself fairly neatly into different subregions, and the format of the book reflects this. The central belt running from Blackburn to Colne was once dominated by textile weaving and is closest to the historical image of the county. To the north of this lie the rural fringes of Pendle and the Ribble Valley, both areas of great beauty. In the north of the county is the historic city of Lancaster and its surrounding area, again both very attractive.

The Preston, South Ribble and Chorley areas are the busy centre of the county, dominated by motorways and more modern industry. In the west lie the areas of the Fylde, Wyre and West Lancashire, with contrasting holiday resorts on the coast and flat market gardening countryside inland.

Each of these areas has its own crop of 'gems', and all add to the quality of the environment in their own communities, reflecting the county's rich and varied history. (Note the 'county' referred to in this book is the post-1974 administrative unit.)

What constitutes a good 'gem'? It is a valid question, and one that is capable of somewhat different responses. In my case, a gem is a building, structure, location or landform that is either rare or unusual architecturally, or is associated with a fascinating story, particularly one that might not have reached the pages of the history books. Both the well-known and the slightly more off-the-beaten-track locations equally fit into this definition.

The choice that follows in these pages is inevitably a personal one, reflecting what is known to me. There are, of course, many others.

# Visiting Sites Listed in This Book

Many of the locations listed in this book are not tourist attractions in their own right, but can be seen, externally at least, without paying an admission fee. Many are visible from the public highway or from other freely accessible areas. A few might require payment of an admission charge. Most can be seen by those with differing abilities.

Postcode information is provided for those using satnav systems; however a word of caution is needed here. Locations in open countryside often have no postal address, and the available postcodes will cover a wide area and will not lead you to the exact site, so be prepared for some local searching using my directions and a Lancashire street atlas!

# Gems of the Lancaster Area

## 1. Lancaster Castle

Lancaster Castle is undoubtedly the best-known tourist attraction of the city. Owned by Her Majesty the Queen as the Duke of Lancaster, it has a long and illustrious history and is in a very attractive area, surrounded by Georgian buildings with Lancaster Priory, a Roman bathhouse and the quayside Maritime Museum just a short walk away.

The site was used for defensive purposes by the Romans. It is thought that the Normans under Roger de Poitou established a timber castle on the site in the 1090s. After de Poitou's departure from England in 1102, the king confiscated the castle, then part of the Honour of Lancaster. During the twelfth and thirteenth centuries, the castle was rebuilt and extended in stone, although the building's long-standing use as a prison has prevented archaeological investigations of its origins being carried

The main gate of Lancaster Castle.

Lancaster Castle's 'Hanging Corner'.

out. The very impressive gatehouse, surely the archetypal gatehouse for any castle, is thought to date from the time John O'Gaunt was Duke of Lancaster.

The castle was used in 1612 for the trial of the Pendle witches, and during this period many Roman Catholic priests would be brought here for trial. The castle changed hands during the Civil War.

Until March 2011, the building's main use was as a gaol and a courthouse, with some high-security trials taking place here, including that of the 'Birmingham Six' (who were later cleared). Guided tours are run through certain parts of the building, dependent on court sittings. The tours include the ten-sided Shire Hall, built in the early nineteenth century and sometimes used as a court, which contains the heraldic shields of the major families of the historic county of Lancashire. A short spell in a lightless and almost airless medieval cell will follow and the tour usually finishes in the Grand Jury Room, an elegant circular room with entrance doors perfectly shaped to fit the walls. With the closure of the prison, gradually more parts of the castle are being opened up for public viewing.

The last execution took place at Lancaster in 1910. 'Hanging Corner', shown in the photograph above, is where they took place in public until 1865, when the practice was moved inside the building. Condemned prisoners would be taken to the 'Drop Room' where they would be prepared for execution, and then brought out of a door – now a window to the gallows located in front of the sealed archway.

*While in the vicinity of the castle, do have a look at the priory church and Roman bathhouse site nearby, and the Maritime Museum on the Quayside.*

*Access: On Castle Hill, which leads off King Street (the northbound A6) via Meeting House Lane. LA1 1YL.*

# 2. Horseshoe Corner, Lancaster

Set into the paving stones at the junction of Market Street, Penny Street and Cheapside (LA1 1LY) in Lancaster's compact city centre is a horseshoe. It is reputedly where the horse carrying John O'Gaunt (1340–99), the 1st Duke of Lancaster, cast one of its shoes.

The metal shoe is renewed periodically and is not the original. The popular story about the horseshoe is now considered a myth, and it is now believed that the shoe marks the site of Lancaster's ancient horse fairs.

*Access: Close by is the City Museum. LA1 1HT.*

# 3. 'The Taj Mahal of the North': Ashton Memorial, Williamson Park, Lancaster

Williamson Park is Lancaster's largest public park. It was first laid out by James Williamson I in 1877 as an unemployment relief project. This was continued by his son, James Williamson II, who developed the family's oil cloth and linoleum business based in the town so much that he became known as the 'Oil Cloth King'.

The younger Williamson was a great philanthropist to the town providing many public buildings and monuments, including the Town Hall. The Ashton Memorial was built in 1907–09 reputedly in memory of his second wife, Jessie, who had died in 1904, although there is doubt over this, with others claiming that it was more of a general family memorial. This may have arisen because Williamson married, for a third time, in 1909. In the meantime, he was given the title Baron Ashton in 1906.

The memorial cost around £87,000 and was designed by Sir John Belcher and his assistant John James Boass. It is located on the highest point of the park, some 497 feet above sea level, on a small plateau known as the 'sixpence'. Local people call it 'The Structure'. At 150 feet high, it dominates the Lancaster skyline and can be easily seen from the nearby M6 motorway.

It is constructed of granite and Portland stone with a copper dome. The floor is made up of white, black and red marble. Nikolaus Pevsner described it as 'the grandest monument in England', and the building is also sometimes as 'The Taj Mahal of the North'.

The building was damaged by fire in 1962 and closed for safety purposes in 1981. Restoration followed in 1985–87 and it is now used either as exhibition space or for small-scale social events.

*Access: The Park is on the eastern side of the city, best reached via Bowerham Road and Coulston Road. LA1 1UX.*

Ashton Memorial,
Williamson Park, Lancaster.

# 4. The Last Surviving Aerial Ropeway, Claughton

Those who grew up near coalfields in the 1960s and 1970s will remember the many aerial ropeways that used to take colliery waste from the pitheads to huge spoil heaps nearby. One features in the 1970s film *Kes* that was shot around the collieries of the Barnsley area.

Other extractive industries used ropeways, including brick production. The Claughton Manor ropeway, which carries shale from quarries on Claughton Moor to brickworks adjoining the main road, is the last operational aerial ropeway in the UK. It was built in 1924, although the brickworks, now part of the Forterra Group, date from 1886.

The quarries are 750 feet above the brickworks, and the ropeway is approximately 1.25 miles long. At the quarry, the shale is tipped into an initial crusher and then into a loading bunker where the ropeway buckets are filled. At the bottom end, the shale is moved by dumper truck to the stocking area.

The ropeway is powered entirely by gravity, with the descending loaded buckets pulling the empty buckets up the hill. A braking system controls the overall speed. The journey time of an individual bucket is thirty-two minutes. The daily capacity of the system is 250 tons. It is an extremely environmentally efficient form of transport.

The brickworks closed due to falling demand in 2009, leaving the ropeway unused, but both reopened in 2014.

A second ropeway, crossing the road nearby, operated until 1990 but was removed some years ago.

*Access: The ropeway crosses the A683 just to the west of the village. LA2 9JY.*

Aerial Ropeway, Claughton Manor brickworks.

The lower 'station' of the aerial ropeway.

# 5. Gray's Seat, near Caton and Arkholme, One of Lancashire's 'Thankful Villages'

The viewpoint here was made famous by the poet Thomas Gray in 1769, when he wrote, 'the Lune serpentizes for many a mile, and comes forth ample and clear, through a well wooded and richly pastured foreground. Every feature which constitutes a perfect landscape of the extensive sort, is here not only boldly marked, but also in its best position'.

Poets and artists in the eighteenth century helped to stimulate interest in the visual landscape. J. M. W. Turner visited here in 1816 while on a sketching tour and local artist John Henderson and Richmond-born George Cuitt also visited.

Gray's Seat, near Caton.

Unfortunately, the view today is heavily obscured by trees that grew up after 1832 when the main road was altered, and is not what Gray and others would have seen.

*

The First World War saw every community in the land send large numbers of young men to fight for their King and Country. Many of these brave souls did not return and have their final resting places in the immaculately kept war cemeteries of northern France and Belgium.

Arkholme sent fifty-nine men to fight, out of a total population of 300. All had been born and bred in the village, including eight who had emigrated to New Zealand but who returned to fight alongside their childhood friends.

Miraculously, all survived the conflict and returned home, making Arkholme a 'Thankful Village', a term first used by author Arthur Mee in the 1930s. There are now thought to be over fifty such villages in the UK, but the quiet and picturesque village of Arkholme is one of only two in Lancashire. The other is Nether Kellet.

Arkholme's fifty-nine men is the largest number sent by any of the Thankful Villages. Their names are commemorated in a 'roll of honour' displayed near the entrance to the church.

*Access: For Grey's Seat, park in the Crook O'Lune car park (signposted from the A683 just to the west of Caton). Take the footpath that leads from the car park down to the old railway. Turn right and cross the river. On the other side, descend by the path to river level and follow the footpath upstream. Turn right after a minute or two onto a path that leads up to the main road. Cross the road – the footpath to Gray's Seat is on your left, and is well signposted. LA2 9HR.*

*Arkholme is on the B6254 roughly halfway between Carnforth and Kirby Lonsdale. The church is close to the end of the unclassified road that leads down to the riverside. LA6 1AU.*

*Below left*: Arkholme Church.

*Below right*: The roll of honour inside Arkholme Church.

# 6. Lindeth Tower, Silverdale – Mrs Gaskell and Crossing the Sands of Morecambe Bay

This tower, sometimes called Gibraltar Tower, was where the Mancunian and Cheshire novelist Elizabeth Gaskell spent many of her summer holidays with her family after discovering the area in the 1850s. It was originally built in 1825 as a holiday retreat by the Preston banker Henry Paul Fleetwood, who was related to the developer of Fleetwood, Sir Peter Hesketh Fleetwood.

The tower is several storeys high, and Mrs Gaskell used the top-floor room as a study. It is thought that the locality 'Abermouth' named in the novel *Ruth* of 1853 was modelled on Silverdale, and that part of the novel *Cranford*, which some claim to be the old name for nearby Carnforth, was also written there.

It is claimed that her greatest joy, when staying here on moonlit nights, was to watch the lines of people crossing Morecambe Sands from Kents Bank to Hest Bank, often accompanied by the four-horse Oversands Coach, guided as it was after dark by a large lantern in the Hest Bank Hotel.

*

Crossing the sands of Morecambe Bay has long been a short cut to reach the Furness Peninsula from the south. The Romans, the monks of Furness Abbey and stagecoaches have all used it, even though it is a treacherous route due to constantly changing quicksands and rapidly approaching tides. In recent times, many Chinese cockle pickers died in one tragic incident.

Lindeth Tower, Silverdale.

The Hest Bank Inn.

In the sixteenth century, the Duchy of Lancaster appointed an official guide to escort travellers over the sands. This post still exists and since 1963 it has been held by the well-known Cedric Robinson. He is paid £15 a year for the privilege, along with the use of a cottage at Kents Bank.

One of the main routes was from Hest Bank to Kents Bank. This route started from the Hest Bank Inn, where the stagecoaches from the south would stop and passengers for the South Lakes or Furness area would transfer to the lightly built Oversands Coach, which was pulled by four horses. For the return journey, the coaches would be guided by a powerful red lantern placed in the large room that overlooks the pub's garden and car park.

Nowadays, coaches crossing the sands are a distant memory, but in the warmer months guided walks can still be booked from Arnside to Kents Bank, to an advertised schedule, taking up to three hours. The crossing should never be attempted without the help of an official guide.

*Access: Lindeth Tower is at the south end of Silverdale, close to the junction of Lindeth Road and Hollins Lane. Follow the sign for 'Jenny Brown's Point' and the tower is visible after a few yards. LA5 0TX.*

*The Hest Bank Inn is via The Crescent, just off the A5105. LA2 6DN.*

# 7. Warton Crags

Warton Crags are an impressive piece of landscape in this part of Lancashire. It is an area favoured by the rock-climbing fraternity.

Fashioned from limestone it is 535 feet high and forms part of the Arnside and Silverdale Area of Outstanding Natural Beauty. Part of the hill is listed as a Site of Special Scientific Interest and two areas are local nature reserves. Various authorities, nature trusts and the Royal Society for the Protection of Birds have ownership.

Warton Crags.

The view from near the summit of Warton Crags looking towards Silverdale.

There is one former quarry and two caves (called Dog Hole and Badger Hole). Rare plants and butterflies can be found on the crags, and they are a breeding ground for peregrine falcons. The remnants of an Iron Age hillfort can be found on the summit.

The views from the summit extend beyond Morecambe Bay to the South Lakes and Ingleborough.

*Access: Crag Road, Warton, LA5 9RY.*

# 8. Leighton Hall

A hall has existed on this site since around 1246. The current Georgian-style hall was built around 1760 for Sir George Towneley of Towneley Hall in Burnley, who had acquired the estate through marriage in the 1750s. The park was laid out around 1763.

The hall was sold in 1805 and in 1822 came into the hands of Richard Gillow, of the Lancaster furniture family. Over the next three years, the façade was refaced with a Gothic appearance using local white sandstone. A three-storey wing designed

*Above left*: View from Leighton Hall.

*Above right*: Falconry display at Leighton Hall.

*Below*: Leighton Hall.

by local architects Paley and Austin, contained guest accommodation and a billiard room was added in 1870.

The property remains in family ownership and retains a family house feel. There are no roped-off areas and it boasts some stunning Gillow furniture, as might be expected. It is open to the public (see website) and a number of events are held in the grounds, including falconry displays. The estate is home to the high brown fritillary, a rare butterfly species, and wild violets.

*Access: Off the A6 north of Carnforth, LA5 9ST.*

# 9. Carnforth Railway Station and 'Brief Encounter'

Carnforth's first railway station was opened in 1846 by the Lancaster & Carlisle Railway. The station became a junction in 1856, and was substantially reconstructed in 1857, 1880 and 1937. During the latter scheme an 890-foot-long platform was constructed serving trains to Barrow-in-Furness, which had the longest single unsupported concrete roof in Britain.

The station's chief claim to fame is that it was used in February 1945 by producer David Lean to film his classic *Brief Encounter*, starring Trevor Howard and Celia Johnson. The location was chosen because it was sufficiently far enough away from the threat of bombing and as a result blackout procedures were no longer necessary. Even so, filming had to be done between 10 p.m. and 6 a.m. so as not to interfere

The central platforms and clock, Carnforth station.

with normal train operations. The station clock on the central platforms featured frequently in the film and became a memorable image. It has recently been restored.

Carnforth station lost significance in May 1970 when the 'main line' platforms were closed during the electrification of the West Coast main line. Most of the buildings became disused and fell into disrepair.

Interest in restoring the station to its former glory and a desire to celebrate its part in the film led in 1996 to the formation of a trust. In late 2000, a £1.5 million project got under way, and the Brief Encounter Visitor Centre opened on 17 October 2003. It is well worth a visit.

Trains still run from the station to Lancaster, Manchester Airport, Barrow and Yorkshire. The possibility of restoring service to the main line platforms gets mentioned occasionally.

*Access: In the centre of Carnforth, LA5 9TR.*

# 10. Eric Morecambe Statue and the Midland Hotel, Morecambe

This bronze statue is by Graham Ibbeson and commemorates one of the UK's best-loved comedians, Eric Morecambe, who was rarely off the television, with his partner 'Ernie' Wise, from the 1960s until his untimely death in 1984. It was unveiled by Her Majesty the Queen on 23 July 1999, and had cost £125,000, some £40,000 being donated by the supermarket chain Morrisons.

The statue is at the top of steps overlooking a purpose-built paved circle surrounded by flower beds. On the ground there are various messages from guests on their shows and sayings of the pair, including their song 'Bring me Sunshine'.

Also inscribed is the fact that their 1977 Christmas show attracted an audience of nearly 29 million viewers – i.e. just about every other person in the country, a number that in this age of multichannel satellite and cable television is unlikely to be challenged.

The statue shows Eric in one of his characteristic poses. Around his neck is a pair of binoculars, as he was also a keen ornithologist.

\*

Nearby is the magnificent art deco Midland Hotel, built by the London Midland & Scottish Railway to a design by Oliver Hill. It opened in July 1933 and replaced an earlier hotel, also called the Midland, which had been built by the 'Little' North Western Railway in 1871.

The hotel is a three-storey curved structure, with a central tower containing the entrance and a spiral staircase. There is a circular café at the northern end of the building.

The convex side faces the sea, and the hotel is clearly designed to complement the curve of the promenade and give guests superb views of the Lake District and its southern shoreline.

*Above left*: Eric Morecambe statue on Morecambe seafront.

*Above right*: The Eric Morecambe statue in its paved circle.

*Below*: Midland Hotel, Morecambe.

Inside are three remarkable carvings by sculptor Eric Gill. On the ceiling of the staircase tower is a bas relief showing the sea god Triton with mermaids. Elsewhere there is a scene from Homer's *Odyssey* and a large carving of a map of Morecambe Bay.

The hotel was requisitioned in 1939 by the Royal Navy, who remained until September 1947. It was then run as a hotel by the British Transport Commission until 1952, when it was sold to private owners. Following a long period of gradual decline, it was spectacularly refurbished by developers Urban Slash in 2008.

*Access: On the seafront. LA4 4NJ is nearby. For the hotel use LA4 4BU.*

# 11. St Patrick's Chapel, Heysham and Viking Graves

This ruined building is one of the oldest surviving Christian sites in north-west England. It was constructed in the eighth century, and enlarged a century or so later. Despite its name, the site is not early enough to be connected with St Patrick, although popular legend has the chapel being founded by him after being shipwrecked here.

Why it was built here is a mystery, a complicated question as parts of the adjoining parish church also date back to the same date. Excavations carried out by the University of Lancaster in the late 1970s revealed many burial sites in the adjoining ground, including a stone carving clearly reused as a grave cover, and a Viking age bone comb. The stone carving is on display in the adjoining parish church.

Close by are two sets of graves that have been cut into the solid rock. Some of these originally had stone or wooden markers. They are quite unique in the UK. Their date is unknown but are thought to be from the Viking era.

*Access: Park in the main village car park, walk up Main Street opposite, and turn left up the path that leads past St Peter's Church, LA3 2RN.*

St Patrick's Chapel,
Heysham.

Viking graves near
St Patrick's Chapel.

# 12. Sambo's Grave, Sunderland Point

African and Afro-Caribbean history, being largely histories of oral tradition, have few places or monuments that they celebrate. This is a small exception.

Sambo (sometimes Samboo) was a black boy who died in 1736, at a time when Sunderland Point was a port for Lancaster. It was one of the stopping places involved in the 'triangular trade' whereby goods were taken from Britain to West Africa and traded for slaves, who were then transported to the Caribbean. The ships then returned to Britain carrying goods such as cotton and tobacco, and maybe a few slaves.

Sambo was one such individual. He died here, reputedly of a broken heart when his master went off on another trip, but more likely when he caught one of the diseases of the Western world against which he would have had little natural

*Above left*: Sambo's Grave, Sunderland Point.

*Above right*: The detailed inscription on Sambo's Grave placed here in 1796.

immunity. He died in the building now called Upsteps Cottage, and was buried here, in the corner of a field next to a salt marsh, in unconsecrated ground as he would have been considered a heathen.

The grave remained unmarked until 1796 when a local schoolmaster raised some money for the metal memorial that contains his poetic epitaph. Nowadays, the grave also contains many mementos left by local school children.

I pondered for a time whether to include this gem in the book. After all, the word 'Sambo' has acquired a derogatory meaning over the years, even predating the 1899 book *Little Black Sambo*, which is actually set in India and portrays the characters favourably, but which has fallen from grace because of the connotations of the names used in it. To help me settle the matter, I spoke to a couple of Afro-Caribbean friends. Their responses were 'It is his name, so who has the right to deny him his name or his little place in history?', and 'That's part of my history, it has got to go in the book'.

*Access: By road, signposted from Overton, but beware that the road is submerged by water at high tides, and you can easily get cut off. Once at Sunderland Point, park and walk through the village. A signpost will take you down a path to the right. At the far end turn left and Sambo's grave is in the field on your left after about a minute's walk. To avoid any risk of being stranded by the tides, park at Potts Corner, accessed via Middleton. Walk along the shore line for about half an hour until you reach Sunderland Point. LA3 3HS.*

# Gems of the Ribble Valley

## 13. Chipping and Slaidburn: Two Picturesque Villages, Two Interesting Pubs in the Forest of Bowland

This public house, built in 1758, is reputedly the most haunted pub in Lancashire. It is haunted by the ghost of Lizzie Dean, a pretty and pleasant scullery maid who liked to dress in colourful clothing. In 1835, she had the misfortune to fall in love with a local lad, who proposed to her to have his 'wicked way' with her.

Thus satisfied, he then proverbially 'dumped' her, and proposed instead to her best friend, who, against Lizzie's wishes, agreed to marry him.

Poor Lizzie could not bear to see this, and on the day of the wedding at the local church she made her way up to the pub's attic, which overlooked the churchyard. There, she wrote a suicide note, and promptly hung herself. In her note, she asked to be buried near the church entrance, so that 'my lover and my best friend will have to walk past my grave every time they go to church'.

The Sun Inn, Chipping.

Another version of the story has an afternoon wedding being set for Lizzie. On the morning of her big day she goes up to the attic to change, only to see her lover marrying her best friend in the morning.

The grave is near to the old entrance to the church, and shows that she died on 5 November 1835. Many 'sightings' and other ghostly goings-on have been reported in the building by visitors and staff ever since.

\*

The Hark to Bounty Inn is the focal point of the very pretty village of Slaidburn, nestled in the Forest of Bowland, an area of great beauty. From 1250, the Chief Court of Bowland, or Halmote, was held in the inn, in the old courtroom, which still contains its original oak furnishings. It was here that tenants came to pay their rents and to take part in the forest courts.

As the only court between Lancaster and York, it was used by visiting justices from the fourteenth century. Cromwell is said to have used it, and it remained in use as a court until 1937.

The inn was called 'The Dog' for a long time, but in 1875 the local hunt gathered there and a visiting squire, so elated on hearing the sound of his own dog (called 'Bounty') outside, exclaimed 'Hark to Bounty' so wholeheartedly that it was adopted as the pub's new name.

The Hark to Bounty Inn, Slaidburn.

The Trough of Bowland, north of Dunsop Bridge.

Another version puts the name change as taking place in 1861, with the Revd Wigglesworth making the exclamation.

The Forest of Bowland is well worth exploring. It is an Area of Outstanding Natural Beauty and parts are Sites of Special Scientific Interest. Only parts are actually forested, the remainder of which a mixture of gritstone fells, peat moorland and deeply incised valleys. Its highest point is Ward's Stone, 1,841 feet above sea level. The area known as the Trough of Bowland divides the forest into two upland areas.

It contains the geographical centre of Great Britain, north of the village of Dunsop Bridge. A visitor centre is located in Beacon Fell Country Park.

*Access: The Sun Inn - at the junction of Windy Street and Talbot Street, in the centre of Chipping. PR3 2GD.*

*The Hark to Bounty Inn is on Town End, close to its junction with Church Street in Slaidburn. BB7 3EP.*

*The Bowland Visitor Centre is at Beacon Fell Road, north east of Goosnargh, PR3 2NL.*

# 14. Roman Ribchester

Cheshire has Chester as its reminder of the Romans; in Lancashire this function falls to the pleasant village of Ribchester, on the banks of the Ribble.

The Romans first established a fort here in AD 72–73 as part of a series of forts built across northern Britain. They usually started out as turf and timber structures, but in Ribchester's case it had been rebuilt in stone by the middle of the first century. The first occupants were a cavalry unit from Asturias in southern Spain. By the end of the second century, they had been replaced by a unit from Hungary, and by this time the surrounding settlement, or *vicus*, had become quite significant, including granaries, two temples and a bathhouse. From this time, however, the importance of the fort began to decline and it was finally abandoned in the fourth century.

Apart from a rampart outside the west side of the church and the Roman bathhouse behind the White Bull Inn, there is little to see of the Roman fort and

Roman museum, Ribchester.

*vicus* today as they are either buried (partly under St Wilfrid's Church) or have been washed away by the changing course of the nearby river.

The museum here was first opened in 1915 by Margaret Greenall, a member of the Warrington brewery family who recognised Ribchester as an important Roman site. The museum was extended in the 1960s and partly rebuilt in the late 1980s. A complete redevelopment was finished in 2001, enabling it to hold a comprehensive collection of Roman finds from the area. Included is a replica of the famous cavalry helmet discovered in 1796 as part of the Ribchester Hoard. The helmet is regarded as the best preserved Roman helmet found in England and is now in the British Museum.

*

The White Bull Inn is a sturdy stone building (dated 1707) that is surrounded by old weavers' cottages and guarded by a crude wooden carving of an elongated white bull on top of a porch. This is supported by four Tuscan pillars taken from the ancient Roman fort, said to have been recovered from the bed of the river. It is thought that the four columns came from the tepedarium of the Roman baths.

In the late eighteenth century, the pub also served as the local courthouse for many years with one of its rooms used for holding prisoners.

The pub was patronised by members of the Channel 4 series *Time Team* during their three-day visit to the village in September 1993.

*Access: The museum is on the south side of the village, just off Church Street. PR3 3XS. The White Bull Inn is on Church Street, PR3 3XP.*

The White Bull Inn, Ribchester.

# 15. Almshouses and Interesting Churches at Stydd, Ribchester

These lovely almshouses at Stydd were built in 1728 under the terms of the will of local landowner John Shireburne, who wished to build 'a good almshouse on his estate at Stydd for five poor persons to live separately therein'.

The building is a mixture of styles, and has been described by Pevsner as 'very curious and engaging'. The front façade appears Italian, with a gallery that allows residents to sit out under cover. All this is tacked on to the basic shape of a traditional Lancashire farmhouse.

For many years, the almshouses were mainly occupied by Roman Catholic widows and spinsters, 'living separately with coals and allowances'. In 1990, the almshouses were restored and now comprise four flats, administered by the Eaves Brook Housing Association, part of the Manchester and District Housing Association.

\*

Despite the religious persecution that followed the Reformation, the Roman Catholic faith always remained strong in Lancashire, and it was practised by many of the local landowning families.

Almshouses, Stydd.

The Church of St Peter and St Paul, Stydd.

The local Walmsley family were Catholics. In the eighteenth century, they leased land at Stydd firstly to Bishop Petre, and after his death to his chaplain, Father William Fisher. Father Fisher arranged for the building of the Church of St Peter and St Paul, further up Stydd Lane, in 1789, some two years before such buildings were officially permitted under the Second Catholic Relief Act. In common with other Catholic churches built at this time, it has the simple appearance of a barn.

It was extended in 1877 and renovated in 1989.

*

At the top end of Stydd Lane is the small medieval Church of St Saviour, which is almost untouched by later renovations. Its exact date and origins remain a mystery. The earliest parts appear to date from the late Norman era (*c.* 1190). During this period, it is thought that a small religious community or 'hospital' existed here, possibly to tend to pilgrims passing through. One suggestion is that the 'hospital' existed to care for the victims of leprosy.

By 1292 the site was controlled by the Knights Hospitallers of the Order of St John of Jerusalem. Whether the religious community still existed then, and if so, for how long is not known. By the fourteenth century, the property was being let out on condition that the tenant maintained the chapel, any other buildings of the 'hospital' by now having disappeared.

After the Dissolution of the Monasteries, the property was sold, but the obligation to hold services in the chapel remained, and burials continued in the churchyard up to the late eighteenth century. By the mid-nineteenth century, the chapel was in considerable decay. A major restoration was instigated by the Rev Samuel Sidebotham, Vicar of Ribchester, in 1925, the costs being met by parishioners and friends together with a contribution of £40 from the Incorporated Church Building Society. Further restoration took place in 2005.

Inside, the church is very basic, with a plain rectangular shape and a stone-flagged floor. The windows appear to date from different periods and there is evidence of a balcony in the form of a blocked door, which possibly led to other earlier buildings. The font and pulpit are from the sixteenth and seventeenth centuries respectively. There are a number of gravestones including that of Bishop Francis Petre, who was buried in 1775.

*Access: The almshouses are on Stydd Lane, which is off the B6245 (Blackburn Road) on the eastern edge of Ribchester. PR3 3YQ.*

St Saviour's Church, Stydd.

Interior view of St Saviour's Church.

# 16. Catholic Lancashire: Stonyhurst College and Whalley Abbey

Stonyhurst College was founded in St Omer (Belgium) in 1593 as an expatriate English Catholic school, as such schools were not allowed in England at the time. It moved at a later date to Bruges, then Liege and then finally to Stonyhurst in 1794 when the existing sixteenth-century manor house was donated with 30 acres of land by Thomas Weld.

Substantial extensions took place in the nineteenth century, including a seminary (now St Mary's Hall), an observatory (built in 1866 and now back in use) and a meteorological station. By the start of the twentieth century, it was not only the largest Catholic college in England, it was also one of the largest houses in the north-west. Further extensions have followed since the 1950s.

Main frontage of Stonyhurst College.

It became co-educational in 1999 and has just over 700 pupils including its preparatory school. Since 2006 it has been the only Jesuit-inspired school in England.

Stonyhurst has a significant reputation and has produced notable staff and alumni, including three saints, seven archbishops and a signatory to the American Declaration of Independence, among others.

There are one or two public open weekends a year (see website for details).

\*

Whalley Abbey has its origins from 1296 when the Cistercian house at Stanlow decided to move here after a series of misfortunes at their original site. Progress was slow with the foundation stone not being laid until 1330. The abbey church was completed in 1380, but the main range of buildings was not finished until the 1440s, with the gatehouse (now under the care of English Heritage) being added in 1480.

The abbey was dissolved in 1537 and sold privately in 1553. Some of the buildings were demolished and replaced by a large house, now a retreat and conference centre. The remaining buildings slowly disappeared over the years, although the foundations are visible. The site was taken over by the Anglican Church in 1923 and it is currently administered by the diocese of Blackburn. An admission charge is payable.

*Access: Stonyhurst College, off Whalley Road (B6243) Clitheroe. Use BB79QB on the public open days.*

*Whalley Abbey is accessed via Church Lane and The Sands, Whalley, BB7 9SS.*

The Sodality Chapel, Stonyhurst College.

Part of the Cloister and surviving wall of the Refectorium, Whalley Abbey.

# 17. Elaborate Family Tombs, Great Mitton, and Bolton-by-Bowland

The church of All Hallows, Great Mitton, is one of the finest medieval churches in the north of England, parts of which date from 1270.

Of particular interest is the fifteenth-century chancel screen believed to have come from nearby Sawley Abbey. The Shireburne Chapel was built for the local gentry family, and replaced an earlier chapel in 1594. It is divided from the chancel by an Elizabethan screen. Set in the floor is a wooden trap door that covers entry to their burial vault.

The chapel contains an excellent group of alabaster tombs, the earliest dating from 1594. Although the effigies show the family in normal dress of the period, all are carved lying recumbent, hand on heart, like medieval knights. The main effigies are those of Richard Shireburne, who died in 1594, and his wife Maud. They lie side by side, him in full armour and she in petticoats. On the wall opposite is a monument with figures in a kneeling position before a prayer desk. These are Sir Richard's son, who died in 1629, and his wife Catherine. To their left are three altar tombs to the succeeding generations, namely Richard (d. 1668), Richard (d. 1689), his wife Isabel (d. 1693) and their son, Richard, who died in 1690. These three tombs were carved by William Stanton of Holborn, and cost £153 in 1699.

The most recent carving, also by Stanton, is of a young boy of nine also called Richard, grandson of Richard and Isabel, who died in 1702 after eating poisonous berries. He is carved standing, surrounded by tokens of death in the form of a skull, crossbones and weeping cherubs.

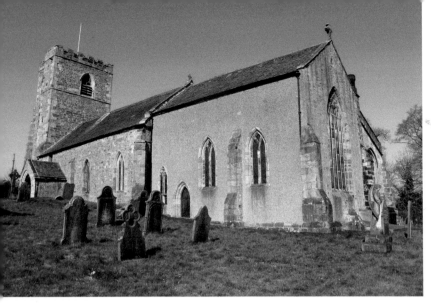

All Hallows
Church, Great
Mitton.

The Shireburne
Chapel inside
All Hallows
Church.

Bolton-by-Bowland is one of Lancashire's most attractive villages, having two village greens, a stone cross and village stocks.In the fifteenth-century parish church of St Peter and St Paul lies this remarkable limestone tomb to the Pudsay family. On it are carved the figures of Sir Ralph Pudsay, his three wives, and their twenty-five children.

Around its base is a brass strip inscribed with the following: 'Ye tomb of Sir Ralph Pudsay Kt Lord of Bolton ye faithful adherent of King Henry VI whom he sheltered at Bolton Hall after ye battle of Hexham AD 1463 was restored by his descendant and heir Pudsay Dawson of Hornby Castle Esq AD 1857. Penser peu de sol'.

The Pudsay Tomb in
Bolton-by-Bowland Church.

On the top of the monument is the engraved figure of Sir Ralph, in full armour, with his three wives, Matilda, Margaret and Edwina. In the lower folds of each woman's dress is a Roman numeral indicating how many children she bore of Sir Ralph (respectively six, two and seventeen).

*Access: All Hallows Church is just off the B6246, to the west of Whalley, BB7 9PH.*
    *The parish church of Bolton-by-Bowland is on the northern side of the main road through the village. BB7 4NP.*

# 18. Lower Hodder or 'Cromwell's' Bridge, Great Mitton

There are two bridges that cross the River Hodder here. The most recent was built in 1826 and is a substantial construction, with piers and parapets.

The older bridge, just downstream, is a three-arched structure built by Sir Richard Shireburne in 1562. It is called Cromwell's Bridge because it is reputed that he passed over it in 1648 before meeting the Royalists in battle at Preston, though this story is disputed.

Lower Hodder or 'Cromwell's Bridge', Great Mitton.

Close to the bridge, Cromwell called a Council of War to discuss how to get his cannon across the narrow bridge.

The old bridge can still be crossed, but not having any parapets it is only for those possessing courage and a head for heights!

*Access: On the B6243, about a mile to the west of Great Mitton. BB7 9PW is nearby.*

# 19. Browsholme Hall

Browsholme (pronounced 'Broozum') Hall is said to be the oldest inhabited house in Lancashire. Although a house has existed here since around 1380, the present building dates from around 1507, with further extensions up to 1603. A garden was added in 1674.

The west wing was rebuilt in 1804/05 and the grounds were improved around this time. The building was opened to the public from the previous year, and significant improvements have been carried out from the 1970s onwards.

The hall has been in the ownership of the Parker family throughout its history and on busy days you are likely to be addressed by a family member on part of the tour. The house retains an atmosphere of a family home, and modern furniture sits alongside antiques, paintings and drawings, some drawn by a past family member. (Check the website for opening hours.)

*Access: Via Clitheroe Road, Clitheroe, BB7 3DE.*

Browsholme Hall.

# 20. Clitheroe Castle

A castle has existed at Clitheroe since the eleventh century, when a motte-and-bailey castle, probably a timber structure, was erected by Roger de Poitou, one of William the Conqueror's followers. Its position was advantageous, being located on the top of a natural limestone outcrop 35 metres high.

The present structure was built in 1186 by Roger de Lacey and is said either to be the smallest keep in the country or the second smallest. It was originally surrounded

General view of Clitheroe Castle.

by a curtain wall and other buildings, including a chapel dedicated to St Michael, but these have now largely disappeared. The castle served as an administrative centre until the early nineteenth century and was the seat of the Lords of Bowland. Besieged by the Scots on one occasion, it is thought that Henry VI was imprisoned here during the Wars of the Roses. Towards the end of the Civil War, its Royalist garrison fled after Prince Rupert's defeat at the Battle of Marston Moor.

The castle was bought by the local authority in 1919, from Lord Montague, to serve as a memorial to those of the town killed in the First World War. Clitheroe Castle Museum operates in one of the adjoining Victorian buildings and is well worth a visit.

The large hole in one of the keep's walls was part of the 'slighting' done in 1649 after the Civil War in order to prevent it being used as an effective military installation. There is no truth in the rumour that the hole was caused by the Devil throwing a large rock at the Castle from Pendle Hill!

In the rose garden on the western side of the castle can be found this turret, which formerly came from the Houses of Parliament, built between 1840 and 1854. It was presented by Captain Brass in 1937. A separate plaque was erected by public subscription after his death in August 1945.

Captain Sir William Brass, Baron Chattisham of Clitheroe, was the town's MP from 1922 to 1945. In 1937, he paid for the layout of the castle gardens in celebration of the Coronation of King George VI.

*Access: At the junction of Moor Lane (B6243) and Castle Gate, in the centre of the town. BB7 1BA.*

*Below left*: The damage caused to Clitheroe Castle in 1649.

*Below right*: The Parliamentary Turret, Clitheroe Castle Gardens.

# Gems of Burnley and Pendle

## 21. The Leeds & Liverpool Canal

The Leeds & Liverpool Canal runs through the heart of Lancashire and was one of the transport arteries that helped the towns along its route develop. The canal has attractive stretches both in open countryside and along many of its urban miles. Of the many points of interest, just a couple will suffice.

The canal passes through Burnley on a high embankment some 60 to 65 feet high called the 'Straight Mile'. Constructed between 1796 and 1801, it is actually only three quarters of a mile long.

The 'Straight Mile' on the Leeds & Liverpool Canal, Burnley.

Foulridge Tunnel.

Several miles north-east is Foulridge Tunnel. This is 1,640 yards long and is sometimes referred to as the 'Mile Tunnel'. It was designed by Robert Whitworth, the canal's engineer, took five years to build and cost £20,000.

The tunnel has no towpath and is not wide enough for two boats to pass. Horse-drawn barges had to be 'legged' through, whereby a couple of men would lie on their backs on the boat deck and 'walk' the boat along the roof. A steam tug was introduced in 1886 after a legger died. This was later replaced by a diesel tug that operated until 1937. Traffic was then controlled by a telephone system until 1963 when a traffic light system controlled by time switches was installed.

In 1912, a cow named 'Buttercup' fell into the canal at the southern end of the tunnel. For some reason she decided to swim through the tunnel to its northern end, where she was helped out and revived with alcohol. Buttercup's fame was celebrated for many years in a photograph that hung in the 'Hole in the Wall' public house, which stood in the village centre. Unfortunately, the pub closed in 2006 and was demolished in 2009. Local enquiries failed to elicit the current whereabouts of the photograph.

*Access: The 'Straight mile' runs between Finsley Gate and Ormerod Road on the eastern side of Burnley town centre. Access to the canal towpath is easy. BB11 2HE.*

*Foulridge Tunnel is best seen from Foulridge Wharf, via Warehouse Lane, which is off the B6251, close to its junction with the A56. BB8 7PP.*

# 22. Gawthorpe Hall and Towneley Hall, Burnley

Gawthorpe Hall was built around a defensive structure erected in the fourteenth century. In August 1600, work started on extending it. Remodelling took place from 1850 by architect Sir Charles Barry and the interior boasts impressive ceilings, panelling and a long gallery.

Built and owned by the Kay-Shuttleworth family, it was gifted to the National Trust in 1972, five years after the death of the last occupant, Rachel Kay-Shuttleworth. Rachel was passionately interested in textiles and amassed during her lifetime what has been described as 'the finest collection of textiles outside the Victoria and Albert Museum', which is now administered by a separate trust. The collection totals some 30,000 items spanning five centuries and originating from across the globe. Some of it is on display in the hall.

The National Trust describe it as 'An Elizabethan gem in the heart of industrial Lancashire'. It is currently managed by Lancashire County Council.

Gawthorpe Hall, near Burnley.

Towneley Hall, Burnley.

Burnley's other hall is the municipally owned Towneley Hall, which stands in its own park on the south-east side of the town. Dating from the fourteenth century, it was the home of the catholic Towneley family for over 500 years before being sold to the local authority in 1901. Since then it has operated as the town's museum and art gallery.

Exhibits include the fifteenth-century vestments from Whalley Abbey and, in the chapel, a finely carved altarpiece made in Antwerp in 1525.

*Access: Gawthorpe Hall is off Burnley Road, Padiham, BB12 8UA.*
*Towneley Hall is off Todmorden Road (A571), BB11 3RQ.*

# 23. Bancroft Mill Engine, Barnoldswick

This preserved steam engine powered the last of thirteen mills to be built in Barnoldswick. It was in continuous service from the mill's opening in 1920 until closure in 1978. The current museum opened in 1982 and is run by volunteers.

*Above*: The main flywheel, Bancroft Mill, Barnoldswick.

*Right*: 'Mary Jane', the low-pressure cylinder, Bancroft Mill.

At the height of production, the mill produced some 200,000 yards of cloth a week from some 1,250 weaving looms. For the technically minded, the engine is a cross compound Corliss valve condensing steam engine. The power was transferred to the looms via a shaft some 263 feet long, fed from the 16-foot flywheel, the engine being 600 horsepower.

The engine has high- and low-pressure cylinders, affectionately named 'James' and 'Mary Jane', respectively.

A second engine is currently being restored. Known as the 'Bradley' engine, it ran at the Corn Lane Mill, Low Bradley, Skipton, from 1901 to 1978.

*Access: Located on Gillians Lane, on the south side of the town. BB19 5QR.*

# 24. Clarion House, Roughlee

This is the last surviving Clarion House in the UK. Its activities originated in a cottage rented in 1899 subsequently transferred to a farmhouse in 1903. The current house was built by the Nelson Independent Labour Party in 1912.

The Independent Labour Party was founded in 1892, and predates the current Labour Party by some fourteen years. Its aims and purposes were broadly similar but not identical to the Labour Party, with which it was affiliated for many years. It had its own MPs until after the Second World War, but after declining membership its separate existence ended in 1975.

The Clarion House, Roughlee.

The growth of early socialist parties contributed to a similar growth in the pursuit of cycling in the late Victorian and early Edwardian eras, allowing easier access to the countryside and outdoor recreation in general. A national Clarion Club was formed in 1895 and still exists.

A network of Clarion Clubs or Houses grew up around the country, sited either on the edges of towns or in suitable destination venues for the new groups of cycling socialists. The clarion – meaning 'to proclaim loudly' – represented a socialist ideal of a commonwealth where cooperation and fellowship prevailed and material greed was absent.

The network of Clarion Clubs gradually disappeared alongside the decline of the Independent Labour Party, but this building continues and thrives as a sole reminder of the movement's aims. It is open to the public every Sunday.

*Access: On Jinny Lane, the road leading from Roughlee towards Newchurch-in-Pendle. BB12 9LL.*

# 25. Stansfield Tower, Blacko

This tower was built in 1890 by Jonathan Stansfield, a local grocer who wished to give himself a view over Ribblesdale. Unfortunately, the tower turned out to be too short to achieve this. Despite this, it probably provides some fine views over the surrounding countryside.

Stansfield Tower, Blacko.

Constructed to a circular shape in rough stone, the tower had a stone internal staircase via an access doorway (now blocked). The tower, sometimes referred to as Blacko Tower, was refurbished in 1950, and in 1964 was whitewashed anonymously one night.

It is claimed to be the site of Malkin Tower, the home of one of the so-called Pendle witches, and was demolished soon after the infamous trial of 1612. However, more recent opinions put Malkin Tower a short distance away to the north-east, part of the current Malkin Tower Farm.

*Access: Entry to Stansfield Tower is not possible as the land is privately owned. On the eastern side of the A682 north of Barrowford. A closer view can be obtained from the network of public footpaths that lead westwards off Gisburn Old Road, which leads northwards off the minor road that runs between Blacko and Barnoldswick. BB9 6NF is nearby.*

# 26. Pendle 'Witch' Country

St Mary's Church in Newchurch-in-Pendle is a very attractive church in an equally attractive village, perched on the side of Pendle Hill. A chapel of ease was originally established here in 1250, with a later chapel dedicated in 1544. The present tower

St Mary's Church, Newchurch-in-Pendle.

was restored in 1653, and again in 1712. The main part dates from around 1740, although the walls were extended in height in 1816–17 to incorporate a gallery into the church.

On the west face is an oval carving that resembles a window, above which is a dripstone. Locally the 'window' is known as the 'Eye of God', being reputedly provided to protect worshippers from witches. There is no recorded purpose behind its construction, which remains a matter for conjecture.

To the right of the church entrance is the Nutter family gravestone, dating probably from the late seventeenth century. It contains a skull and crossbones together with an hourglass. Despite this, it is not thought to be the grave of Alice Nutter, one of the Pendle witches, who could not have been buried in consecrated ground.

In August every year, the church holds its annual Rushbearing Ceremony when rushes are scattered on the floor and in the pews. Villagers process through the village carrying rushes, singing hymns and accompanied by a brass band. After the crowning of the Rushbearing Queen, there is a short church service followed by high tea in the nearby school.

The 'Eye of God', St Mary's Church.

Ceramic plaque symbolising Katherine Hewitt, whose husband had been a clothier, Pendle Sculpture Trail.

'Three bats in flight', Pendle Sculpture Trail.

Roger Nowell, the magistrate, Pendle Sculpture Trail.

To the north of Newchurch lies the equally attractive village of Barley. From here can be found the Pendle Sculpture Trail. Set in Aitkin Wood this contains a number of sculptures by local artists commemorating the Pendle witches executed at Lancaster including a life-sized model of the chief witch finder, magistrate Roger Nowell. Together with the sculptures are ceramic plaques symbolising each of the

Pendle Heritage Centre.

ten people accused of witchcraft in 1612. The trail dates from 2012. The whole trail is very atmospheric, though rather steep in places and not suitable for wheelchairs or pushchairs.

\*

Those wanting to explore the Pendle witches story further should visit the Pendle Heritage Centre in nearby Barrowford. Opened in 1977 in Park Hill, a former farmhouse dating from 1661, the building was the home of the Swinglehurst and Bannister families, and yes, the late Sir Roger Bannister – who first broke the four minute mile record – was a descendant.

The building today is the starting point of the Pendle Witches Walk and the home of Pendle Art Gallery.

*Access: St Mary's Church is in the centre of the village. BB12 9JR.*

*For the Pendle Sculpture Trail use the main car park in Barley (BB12 9JX) and take the footpath that leads up Barley Lane for about a mile to the start of the trail. The trail is steep in places. The whole walk takes around two to three hours.*

*Pendle Heritage Centre is located on Colne Road, BB9 6JQ.*

# 27. Wycoller Country Park

Wycoller Country Park is well worth seeking out and is a very atmospheric spot. Its centrepiece is Wycoller Hall. The exact date when the hall was constructed is unknown, possibly as early as 1550. More probably, the hall dates from the late soxteenth or early seventeenth centuries, being gradually extended over the years. It is also thought that the hall was never in fact one single dwelling.

The Cunliffe family were the owners from 1611. The last squire, Henry Owen Cunliffe, carried out a large number of alterations between 1774 and his death in 1818. These alterations included the strange 'keyhole' opening to the side of the fireplace, possibly a cupboard for keeping powdered wigs.

Wycoller Hall, Wycoller Country Park.

The Packhorse or Sally Bridge, Wycoller Country Park.

The estate was broken up after 1818 and one subsequent owner of the hall, the Revd John Roberts Oldham, sold the doors, windows, roofing timber and some stone to support building a mill in Trawden.

It is believed that the hall was used by Charlotte Bronte as the model for 'Ferndene Manor' in her novel *Jane Eyre*. A photograph of the hall was used to represent Ferndene in the 1887 Haworth edition of the novel. More recently, the hall's surroundings have featured in television period dramas. The Aisled Barn nearby is also well worth visiting.

Three quite interesting bridges cross the Wycoller Beck as it passes through the village. The Pack Horse Bridge is twin arched and in the village centre. Thought to date from the thirteenth century, it was probably built by the abbey that controlled land in the area. It is also called the Sally Bridge, after Sally Owen, the mother of the last squire of Wycoller.

The Clapper Bridge, which dates from the late eighteenth or early nineteenth century, consists of simple flat stone slabs. It is also known as the Hall, Weavers or Druids Bridge.

The Clapper, Hall, Weaver's or Druid's Bridge, Wycoller Country Park.

The Clam Bridge is further up the Beck. It is believed to be of neolithic origin and is a single long stone laid rather precariously over the water. Damaged by flash floods in May 1989 and August 1990, it has been repaired.

*Access: Access to Wycoller is via minor roads off the Colne to Trawden road (B6250). Park at the visitor car park at the top of the hill and proceed on foot as close vehicular access is not allowed. BB8 8SY.*

# 28. Wallace Hartley Memorial, Colne

This memorial, which contains a bronze bust of its subject, celebrates the leader of the band that played to passengers as the *Titanic* sank in the icy waters off Newfoundland on the night of 14 April 1912. The band has become famous for continuing to perform on deck in an attempt to calm the passengers, playing almost until the ship sank. They all lost their lives in doing so.

Wallace Henry Hartley was born in Colne in 1878 and at an early age had learned to play the violin, his father being choirmaster at the town's Bethel Chapel. By fifteen he was giving solo performances and went on to lead an orchestra in Bridlington. In 1909, after a short spell as a bank clerk, he began working on Cunard steamships, being employed by the agency C. W. & F. N. Black of Liverpool, who supplied musicians for the major shipping lines.

In April 1912, Hartley was assigned to the *Titanic*'s inaugural transatlantic trip. Although reluctant to leave his fiancée, Maria Robinson, to whom he had recently become engaged, he decided that working on this prestigious trip would be good for future work opportunities. Strictly speaking, Wallace and the rest of the band were never employees of the White Star Line, as they were 'contractors' and would have had accommodation on the ship as passengers.

*Above left*: Wallace Hartley Memorial, Colne.

*Above right*: The largest flagstone in Lancashire outside Colne Town Hall.

The last piece the band played on the stricken ship has been popularly regarded as the hymn 'Nearer my God to Thee', to the tune 'Proprior Deo', but other accounts say a dance tune ('Autumn') was played, and the matter is debated.

Hartley's body was recovered some two weeks later and was brought back to England. Over 1,000 people attended his funeral in Bethel Chapel on 18 May 1912 and 40,000 watched the funeral procession. This memorial was erected in 1915 in the grounds of the then rectory. A separate monument, with a carved violin at its base, is in the cemetery on Keighley Road.

*

Colne also has what is reputedly the largest flagstone in Lancashire, although the claim is disputed. This flagstone measures 10 feet by 9 feet and is said to weigh some 2 tons and is 5 inches thick.

It was placed here when the Town Hall was built in 1883–84, to a design by Alfred Waterhouse, the designer of Manchester Town Hall. The team of men who laid the flagstone included a big Norwegian, Lars Larson. Before coming to Colne he had been a seaman, but found employment as a flagger. In 1923, he adopted an English name Lewis Marinus Lawson.

*Access: On the northern side of Albert Road, just to the west of the town centre. BB8 0AE.*

*Colne Town Hall is further up the hill on Albert Road in the town centre. BB8 0AQ.*

# Gems of Blackburn with Darwen, Hyndburn and Rossendale

## 29. Jubilee Tower, Darwen

Often called 'Darwen Tower', this was built to celebrate both the Diamond Jubilee of Queen Victoria in 1897 and the victory of local people in regaining access to the surrounding moorland. It opened on 24 September 1898.

Jubilee Tower, Darwen.

The moors above Darwen had long been open to the public including packhorse operators, pedlars, farmers and others. In the 1870s, realising the increasing value of the moorlands for shooting and sporting, the owner and lord of the mjanor, the Revd William Arthur Duckworth, blocked all access.

Local people were enraged and William Ashton, a manager at Eccles Shorrocks' local collieries, decided to lead the opposition and confronted Duckworth's gamekeepers, so clearing the access paths. The matter ended up in court where Duckworth lost and access was restored. In September 1896, Ashton's two sons (Ashton himself had died in 1894) led a procession onto the moorland to celebrate victory.

As might be expected, the tower is mainly a sturdy structure. Access to the top is via a pair of staircases. In 1947, the original wooden turret was blown off by high winds. It was not replaced until 1971, when Bill Lees, then mayor of Darwen, launched an appeal for funds to replace it with a glass and metal structure. The tower closed from October 2000 to April 2002 when restoration works took place.

In November 2010, the turret was again blown off by wind. The local authority entered into discussions with several local firms who offered to undertake the necessary work at cost. The local papers and blog sites were inundated for a time with arguments from Darweners and Blackburn people (there is no love lost between the two) as to who should and who should not pay the cost! A replacement stainless steel dome made by a Darwen firm was carefully placed on the tower by helicopter in January 2012.

*Access: Via Earnsdale Road, off the western side of the A666 north of Darwen town centre. At the end turn right onto Sunnyhurst to reach the car park. Retrace your steps along the road for a short distance to where signposted footpaths lead uphill towards the tower. BB3 1JX.*

# 30. Haworth Art Gallery, Accrington, and Its Amazing Collection of Tiffany Glass

This lovely building was constructed in 1909 by Walter H. Brierley of York as a retirement home for cotton manufacturer William Haworth. Originally called 'Hollins Hill', Haworth died in 1913 and it became Accrington's art gallery in 1921.

Although the exterior is built in a vaguely Tudor style, inside the style is Arts and Crafts, with an oak-panelled entrance hall and main rooms decorated with plaster and carved wooden flowers, birds and animals.

The building's main claim to fame is its famous collection of Tiffany glass, which includes some 140 pieces, perhaps the largest in the world.

Louis Comfort Tiffany (1873–1933) was renowned for producing his 'Favrile' style of glassware in New York and for a time it was extremely fashionable.

Haworth
Art Gallery,
Accrington.

The connection with Accrington comes from Joseph Briggs, a design apprentice at a local calico works, who went to the USA to seek a better life. He worked for Tiffany for around forty years from 1892, eventually finishing up as works manager. Shortly after Tiffany died, by which time the glass was no longer fashionable, Briggs shipped three crates back to his home town and gave it to the local authority. After a period of time, the value of the collection was realised, and in recent decades it has gained the recognition it rightly deserves.

*Access: Located to the south of the town, on Hollins Lane, close to Manchester Road (A680), BB5 2JS.*

# 31. Rhyddings Methodist Church, Oswaldtwistle

This unassuming, mainly rebuilt Methodist chapel may seem an unlikely contender for this book. However it was the place where quite an interesting local history story took place – one where hardened Nazis were seen weeping after the end of the Second World War.

Methodism first came to Oswaldtwistle at the end of the eighteenth century. A number of chapels were built. One, called Hippings Methodist Church, operated within part of a cotton mill. This was replaced by a permanent building, called Mount Pleasant Chapel, built in 1845–46 on the current site and donated by a local factory owner. A Sunday school followed in 1851 and a day school shortly after.

Mount Pleasant Chapel was partly demolished in 1984 and replaced by the present building, which incorporates the ground floor façade of the old building. It is now known as Rhyddings Methodist Church.

Rhyddings
Methodist
Church,
Oswaldtwistle.

From the end of the Second World War until 1949, camps throughout the UK were used for housing German prisoners of war. Many were located near small towns. One such camp was at Stanhill, on land now covered by the M65 motorway near the Hyndburn–Blackburn boundary. The prisoners were kept there for re-education (at first) and then to help out rebuilding the local economy, in many cases working on neighbouring farms.

The prisoners were placed in three categories. The lowest category – non-Nazis – were soon allowed home. The second and third categories, comprising Nazi party members, were kept longer.

From December 1946, limited local fraternisation was allowed. In Oswaldtwistle's case, the minister at Mount Pleasant Chapel, Revd Joseph Howe, also the camp padre, became the driving force in this. He tried to ensure the men he met were treated as honourably as possible. This involved, among other things, inviting them into his own home and those of his congregation. In time, bonds of friendship grew between the prisoners and their hosts.

At Christmas 1946, a group was allowed to sit at the back of the chapel for the annual carol service. At one point the carol 'Silent Night' was sung in German – 'Stille Nacht'. Some of the prisoners were seen weeping, the carol reminding them of Christmases they would have enjoyed at home. It was also a sign that these once hardened men were becoming ready to rejoin the real world.

Some of the Germans didn't return home after the war, but remained in the UK. One of them was the famous Manchester City goalkeeper Bert Trautmann, who had been kept at a similar camp near Ashton in Makerfield until 1948.

The story of the Germans at Oswaldtwistle, and her father's role in this, is told in full in Pamela Howe Taylor's books *Enemies Become Friends* and *The Germans We Trusted*. The subject was also covered in a BBC *Timewatch* documentary, which did full justice to the story.

*Access: Chapel Street, off the south side of High Street (A 678), BB5 3EP.*

# 32. Former Coke Ovens, Aspen Colliery, Oswaldtwistle's 'Fairy Caves'

Close to the canal bank, running roughly north–south, are the remains of three lines of beehive-shaped coke ovens. Built of strong refractory bricks, they are sometimes mistaken for brick kilns.

They formed part of the former Aspen Colliery opened in 1869 by Thomas Simpson & Co. The date the ovens were built is not known precisely, but the 1893 Ordnance Survey map shows two of the banks.

Coal would have been fed in from the top, which was then sealed with fireclay. The ovens were then fired for between two and five days, after which the resulting coke, roughly 5 tons from each oven, would have been carried by small rail tubs to barges waiting in the adjacent canal basin (now partially filled).

A survey of Lancashire collieries in 1918 showed some seventy-nine men working underground and eighteen at the surface in the colliery. The whole complex was abandoned in the 1920s.

The ovens and basin area is now a Scheduled Ancient Monument, the only one in Hyndburn. The local authorities have been proposing restoration for some time and a conservation plan was drawn up in 2003. However, at the time of writing (2018), progress has yet to be made on the ground.

Local children refer to the ovens as the 'Fairy Caves', and they are often subject to vandalism and other acts of mischief.

*Access: Visible to the north of Blackburn Road (A679) on the northern side of the town. For a closer look, take the track that leads off the road near the junction with Thwaites Road. Cross the canal bridge and follow the canal eastwards for a few minutes. BB5 4NQ.*

The 'Fairy Caves', Oswaldtwistle.

# 33. Fitzpatrick's Temperance Bar, Rawtenstall

Temperance bars began to be established after 1832 when Joseph Livesey, a cheesemaker from Preston, established the temperance movement in response to the widespread consumption of alcohol.

These bars, licensed to open on Sundays, initially advocated a moderate approach towards alcohol consumption and life in general, but later insisted customers 'took the pledge' (of temperance) – i.e. no alcohol consumption whatsoever.

Many towns in the north of England had temperance bars, and were focal points in local communities. There was a strong connection with nonconformist religious movements, particularly Methodism.

Fitzpatrick's first opened in 1891, and was one of twenty-four established by that family, who had emigrated from Ireland the previous decade. They sold non-alcoholic drinks, herbal remedies and their own cordials, brewed to original recipes from Ireland, comprising drinks like sarsparilla, blood tonic (!) and dandelion and burdock. Vimto, the famous Manchester-based drink, was first sold in temperance bars.

This bar remained in the family until 1980, the last fifty or so years being in the hands of Malachi Fitzpatrick, who lived until the age of ninety, and who attributed his longevity to the healthy drinks he brewed.

Due to the influx of modern non-alcoholic drinks and changing social patterns, temperance bars had virtually disappeared by the middle of the twentieth century. Fitzpatrick's survived with a loyal band of customers, and is now run by new owners, who have given it a new lease of life.

The interior is well worth visiting, not only for the award-winning drinks, but also for the bar's genuine antique features. There are organ-looking stops with names like

Fitzpatrick's Temperence Bar, Rawtenstall.

'Wino' and 'Cream Soda', old jars containing herbs and an old copper hot water urn originally from the town's Astoria Ballroom.

*The town's own museum in Whitaker Park is worth a visit, as is the East Lancs Railway, which runs from Rawtenstall to Heywood via Ramsbottom and Bury.*

*Access: At the junction of Bank Street and St Mary's Way in the town centre, BB4 6QS.*

# 34. Ellen Strange Monument, Robin Hood's Well and the Pilgrim's Monument, Holcombe Moor

Robin Hood's Well comprises a spring whose water issues from beneath a large, worn stone capping set against a dry-stone wall by the pathway known as 'Stake Lane'. The water falls into a small pool.

It is likely that this well was used by pilgrims on their way to Whalley Abbey. Researchers have not discovered any references to its original dedication; neither is there any record describing any healing properties attributed to the water.

Just past the well is a gateway. Take the right-hand pathway, which divides after a few minutes' walk, and take the left-hand pathway following the general direction of the flagpole on the horizon. After a further few minutes' walk the memorial to Ellen Strange can be seen.

Robin Hood's Well, Holcombe Moor.

This carved column, containing the outline of a young woman, and the adjacent stone cairn, marks the murder at this spot of Ellen Broadley (née Strange).

The traditional story was that young Ellen, a farmer's daughter, was murdered here by her lover, described as a pedlar. The couple were returning from Haslingden Fair to Ellen's home near Bolton. The murderer was subsequently tried, convicted and hanged at Lancaster, with his body placed on a gibbet at Bull Hill. This story seems to have originated in a ballad written in 1872 by John Fawcett Skelton from Bolton, and was accepted in the locality as late as the 1970s.

The column was erected in 1978 and was carved by Liverpool artist Don McKinlay. It was placed here when locally based theatre group, the Horse and Bamboo Theatre, put on a performance to commemorate the legend. The performance caused some controversy locally as it was said to include an attempt to exorcise the site. These criticisms led to local historians attempting to find out the true story of what happened and the results were published in a booklet by John Simpson.

Ellen had been married to John Broadley, a labourer from Clayton le Moors, for around ten years. Their relationship may have been quite violent. They were paupers, who moved around looking for work. They also frequently visited local hostelries and could have had a violent altercation with one another on the night. After this, Simpson speculates that Ellen tried to make her way over the moors to the family home at Ash Farm, near Hawkshaw, and that Broadley, in a drunken rage, followed her and subsequently killed her.

Broadley was tried for murder, but was acquitted due to the lack of witnesses and the fact that he had first raised the alarm.

Continuing southwards from the Ellen Strange monument takes you along the edge of the Army's Holcombe Moor range (watch out and observe the red flag warnings). Pilgrim's Cross comes into view after a further fifteen to twenty minutes' walk.

The present cross, a square monument, was placed here in 1902 by the vicar of Holcombe to commemorate the old cross said to have stood here since the tenth century. The sides are inscribed with details of the site's history.

Precisely when the old cross disappeared is not known, although its base is said to have been 'willfully destroyed' shortly before the erection of the present structure, sometimes referred to as Whowell's Cross.

Ellen Strange Memorial, Holcombe Moor.

Pilgrim's Cross, Holcombe Moor.

The larger of the stones weighs over 4 tons and was hauled here by a team of fourteen horses and two 'lurries', the journey taking 3.5 hours. The stone had been mined at Fletcher Bank Mill.

*Access: Turn onto Alden Road, which leads southwards from the junction of Holcombe Road (B6375) and Free Lane (B6214). Park about a quarter of a mile up Alden Road and walk through the gateway marked 'Dowry Head'. Turn right onto Moor Road. After a challenging ten to fifteen minute uphill walk, Robin Hood's Well can be seen on the right. BB4 4AE (for where to park your car).*

# 35. Bacup Natural History Museum and the Shortest Street in England

In the mid to late nineteenth century, every town of any merit had its own natural history society, drawn up of (mainly) men interested in their natural environment, its flora, fauna and geology. Some societies set up small museums, many duly evolving into town and municipal museums.

In Bacup's case, both the society and museum survive. The society was formed in 1878 and was run, as now, by volunteers. Its first premises were in a small house on

Bacup Natural History Museum.

Rochdale Road, which became known locally as the 'Bug Club'. The museum had a number of locations over the years, the current one, the former 'Hare and Hounds' pub, being occupied from 1947.

Over the years, the museum's collection has expanded to include local history, military artefacts, mining and industrial archaeology etc. The library has around 2,000 books and copies of Bacup newspapers from 1863.

The museum is open during society meetings on Thursday evenings and also during the day on Easter Saturday.

*

Bacup town centre has been described as the best example of an original mill town existing in the UK. It is a Conservation Area and has been used in a number of television series. It is also the location of Elgin Street, which at just 17 feet 2 inches (5.2 metres) long, lays claim to be the shortest street in England and once named as the shortest in the world in the Guinness Book of Records.

The title, however, was lost in 2006 when it was supplanted by Ebenezer Place in Wick, Scotland. That street had existed since 1883, and had been named in 1887, but had not been recognised as no property had an entrance onto it. This was rectified in 2006 when an additional doorway to an existing property was created.

Elgin Street, too, only serves one property, No. 1, which is not currently occupied.

*Access: The museum is located on Yorkshire Street in the centre of the town. OL13 8AE.*

*Elgin Street is located close to the town centre, off Lord Street, close to the junction with Bankside Street. Although it can be seen from above, direct access is no longer possible as the entrance alleyway is now blocked off. OL13 8HE.*

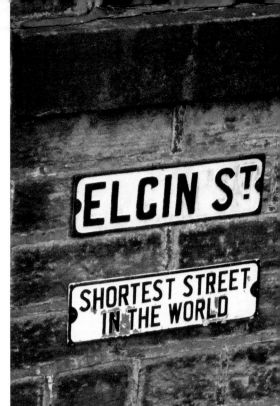

*Above left*: Elgin Street, Bacup.

*Above right*: Street sign, Elgin Street.

# 36. Britannia Coconut Dancers, Bacup

The Britannia Coconut Dancers (or 'Nutters') are one of those curious local customs that thankfully still exist in times of increasing standardisation and globalisation.

They parade every Easter Saturday, performing their dances with the Stacksteads Silver Band, and sometimes with a group playing concertinas. There are eight male dancers, plus a whipper-in, who helps to control traffic. Their processional dance alternates between jogging along the road and a stationary part in which they clap together the wooden 'coconuts' (bobbin tops from the mill) that each dancer has strapped to his hands, knees, and waist.

At certain points, the group stops and performs one or more of five garland dances. Standing in square 'quadrille' formation, each dancer holds a decorated semicircular hoop above his head.

The procession begins annually at 9 a.m. at the former Traveller's Rest public house on the A671 at the boundary with Whitworth. The group dance their way

Britannia Coconut
Dancers, outside the
local fire station, Bacup.

Britannia Coconut
Dancers dancing on the
main road.

along the main road towards the town centre, where they visit local hostelries. If the weather is fine, the procession will split and continue along the roads to the Rawtenstall boundary and the northern edge of the town, finishing around 8 p.m.

The dancers have blackened faces and wear strange colourful costumes. The current 'tradition' dates back to the early 1920s, when a team, based at the Britannia Mill, were taught the dance by the Tunstead Mill Nutters, also from the Bacup area. The Tunstead Mill Nutters celebrated their golden jubilee in 1907, so it is thought that the dance first started in 1857. It is claimed that the tradition has its roots in Moorish, pagan, medieval, mining and Cornish customs.

*Access: At various sites along the A671 and A681. OL13 9SD (for the starting point).*

# Gems of Blackpool, the Fylde and Wyre

## 37. Blackpool Tower

Construction of Blackpool Tower started in 1891 and it opened on 14 May 1894 when some 70,000 people attended. It was the brainchild of Blackpool Mayor John Bickerstaffe (sometimes Bickerstaft) who had visited the Paris Exhibition in 1889 and been impressed by Gustave Eiffel's creation. It was designed by Maxwell and Tuke, prominent Lancashire architects, and cost around £290,000.

Five million bricks, 2,500 tons of iron and 93 tons of cast steel were used in construction. The base of the tower, unlike the Eiffel Tower, is surrounded by a building

Blackpool Tower.

housing other attractions of the complex. Within the four legs is located the long standing Tower Circus. At some 518 feet 9 inches high, the Tower is less than half the height of its Paris counterpart. Despite this, fantastic views can be gained from the top.

At first the Tower was not painted and in 1921–24 it was necessary to renew all the steelwork.

The complex houses a range of attractions, varying over the years. An indoor zoo existed unitl the early 1970s and an aquarium until 2010, when it was replaced by a dungeon-style attraction. At the top of the tower, a 'walk of faith' glass floor panel, some 2 inches thick, was introduced in 1998.

Also notable is the Tower Ballroom, built in 1897–98 to an elaborate Rococo design by theatre designer Frank Matcham. This has featured appearances by many famous dance bands over the years and has been used in a number of television programmes. In 1930 a young Sheffield-born organist called Reginald Dixon was taken on a two-week trial to play the Ballroom's Wurlitzer organ. He became world famous and only retired in 1970. His signature tune – 'Oh! I Do Like to be Beside the Seaside' – became synonymous with Blackpool, the Tower and himself.

The Tower has been owned by many parties over the years.

A similar, though slightly higher, tower existed at New Brighton on the Wirral until just after the First World War, and another was part built at Wembley on the site that is now Wembley Stadium.

*Access: On the Promenade and visible for miles around! FY1 4BJ.*

# 38. Blackpool Tramway

The first tramway in Blackpool started operation on 29 September 1885. The system was initially owned by a private company and operated with the conduit system of current collection. In 1892, the local authority took over, replacing the conduit

Blackpool Tramway, traditional single-decker at Cleveleys, before reconstruction.

system with the more familiar overhead line system in 1899. Further lines were built in subsequent years serving Marton, Layton, Starr Gate, North Station and Gynn Square, where a connection was made with the separately owned and constructed line to Fleetwood. The company that operated the latter was taken over in 1920.

The tramway played a large part in the town's development as a resort. It is particularly helpful during the autumn illuminations season, where it can handle large numbers of passengers. The system carries 7 million passengers each year and is marketed under the slogan 'Blackpool tramway – 11 miles of coastline to explore'. A small number of special illuminated vehicles have been built over the years resembling space rockets, fishing trawlers, western trains etc.

Closure of two routes took place in the 1930s, but the rest of the tramway and fleet were modernised under progressive transport manager Walter Luff. Closure of the remaining street routes took place in 1961–63, leaving just the coastal route from Starr Gate to Fleetwood. Between 1963 and 1992, when Manchester's Metrolink opened, the Blackpool line was the only tramway operating in the UK.

The current route is mainly on its own right of way. The town is also one of only three in the world to operate double-decker tramcars, the others being Hong Kong and Alexandria in Egypt.

From 2009, a major reconstruction took place, allowing for higher speeds, prioritisation at traffic lights and improved disabled access. The character of the tramway was altered considerably by this work. New 'Flexity' tramcars replaced the previous fleet, some of which was disposed of, although a collection of trams has been retained for a 'heritage' service over part of the route in the peak season,

Street running section of Blackpool Tramway in Fleetwood before reconstruction.

One of the new 'Flexity' trams at Starr Gate, Blackpool Tramway.

and others have been modified to run in tandem with the new vehicles. The new tramway started operation in April 2012.

Work on an extension of the system by way of a branch up Talbot Road to reach North Station commenced in 2018.

*Access: Through Blackpool, the line runs mainly along the seafront between Starr Gate and Bispham. From there it continues to Cleveleys and Fleetwood. FY1 4BJ and various.*

# 39. Lytham Windmill and Lytham Hall

Whereas Blackpool Tower is the instantly recognisable symbol of its larger neighbour, smaller and more genteel Lytham relies on its windmill, set in grassy surroundings on the seafront.

The windmill was constructed in 1805 by the local squire and let to a Mr Cookson for a rent of 7 shillings (35 pence) a year. The area around the mill was known as Lytham Marsh. It is thought that some of its machinery came from earlier mills that had existed nearby.

The windmill at Lytham.

The current brick plinth was added around ten years later in order to protect people and animals from being struck by the sails. Some said that it made the windmill look like a candle in a saucer.

After a busy few years, the surrounding area began to be developed as a holiday destination. The noise of the mill's machinery did not fit the town's new image. By 1840 the marsh had been drained and replaced by the level grasslands that exist today. A drying kiln, which had been erected alongside, was removed around 1849.

The mill became an attraction to visitors, who would paste their visiting cards on the inside walls. Sadly, a young boy from Manchester on a school trip clung to one of the sails as it swept past. He lost his grip, fell and was killed.

In the early years of the twentieth century a gas engine was installed to help it compete against new industrialised milling, and continue milling on calm days.

The mill was badly damaged by fire in January 1919, when a severe gale caused the sails to travel round at a rate that could not be controlled. Sparks from the machinery caused the fire, which destroyed the machinery and the mill's top. Following this, the Squire of Lytham, John Clifton, gave the mill to Lytham Corporation. It received some cosmetic restoration, complete with dummy sails, and was put to a number of uses over the years.

Further restorations of the mill took place in 1963 and 1987–89. It now functions as the town's local history museum and is well worth a visit.

*

While in Lytham, do have a look at Lytham Hall. This was built by the Yorkshire architect John Carr in the years 1757 to 1764 for Squire Thomas Clifton, partly incorporating a Jacobean building on the site, which had itself replaced Lytham Priory.

The building has a distinctly Georgian style, with its principal rooms on the ground floor and family accommodation above. It is surrounded by 78 acres of parkland and is described as 'The finest Georgian house in Lancashire'. Like many country houses the house was used as an auxiliary military hospital during the First

World War, and in 1922 the Cliftons ceased living in the property. In 1963 it was sold to an insurance company for use as office accommodation.

Lytham Town Trust bought the building in 1997 with assistance from BAE Systems and it was subsequently leased to the Heritage Trust for the north-west. Both park and house are open to the public (see website for details), and both are currently the subject of restoration proposals.

*Access: Close to the junction of East Beach (A584) and Station Road (B5259). FY8 5LD. Lytham Hall is located on Ballam Road, FY8 4JX.*

# 40. St Cuthbert's Cross, Lytham St Annes

St Cuthbert is thought to have been born near Melrose, in Scotland, of impoverished parents.

He spent several years as a soldier, probably defending the Kingdom of Northumbria against the attacks of King Penda of Mercia. Later, Cuthbert entered the monastery at Melrose, where his devotion became noteworthy.

In 664 he became Prior of Melrose, but was then sent to Lindisfarne to ease the transition to Roman tradition in that house after the Synod of Whitby. In 676 the abbot granted him leave to retire to take up the simple life of a hermit. After several years of austere life on Farne, Cuthbert returned to a more active role in the church, and became Bishop of Lindisfarne.

St Cuthbert's Cross, Lytham.

His consecration was held at York at Easter, 685. He returned to Lindisfarne, but in 686 he resigned his see and returned to Farne Island. He died on March 20, 687.

Cuthbert was buried at Lindisfarne Priory, where his tomb quickly became a magnet for pilgrims. 200 years after his death Lindisfarne was attacked by the invading Danes, so the monks fled to Melrose – and took Cuthbert's remains with them.

One of the places they rested was Lytham, and the stone cross by the cricket ground allegedly marks the spot where his remains rested.

Some have claimed that this is where St Cuthbert is buried, but this story is not now believed, it being only a resting place, not his grave. A gravestone for him exists in Durham Cathedral. Another legend put his final resting place at Crayke Abbey, where he was buried secretly after the arrival of Henry VIII's commissioners. The body was replaced by that of a recently deceased local brother. Today, the legend continues that the true location is known only to twelve monks, its whereabouts only revealed to another monk when one of them dies.

*Access: On the northern side of Church Road, next to the cricket ground, on the western side of the town. FY8 5QL is nearby.*

# 41. Garstang Town Centre

The pleasant town of Garstang is well worth a visit, with several interesting buildings. In front of the Royal Oak Inn stands the Market Cross. Its precise history is not known, but it is thought that the crosspiece was removed during religious unrest. The town was originally granted the right to hold a market by Edward II during the

*Above left*: Market Cross, Garstang.

*Above right*: Town Hall, Garstang.

1300s. This right lapsed and had to be renewed several times but a market is still held on Thursdays, when a bell is traditionally rung at 10 a.m.

Close by stands the Town Hall. The first building was erected in 1680 to acknowledge the grant of borough status for the town. It was destroyed by fire in 1750 and rebuilt five years later. The building suffered a second fire in 1939, when many of the town's historical records were lost.

On the town's western edge runs the Lancaster Canal, which reached Garstang in 1797. Adjoining the large basin is the Tithebarn, which was built around 1720 and is currently a restaurant.

The Tithebarn adjoining the Lancaster Canal, Garstang.

Across the road from the main car park is the Arts Centre, run by the Garstang Town Trust. This was originally the Boys Grammar School, built in 1756 and closed in 1928.

*Access: Off the A6, between Preston and Lancaster. The main car park is at the northern end of the town. PR3 1EB and various.*

# 42. Lighthouses, Fleetwood

The town of Fleetwood owes much of its development to local landowner Sir Peter Hesketh Fleetwood, who risked his wealthy status in the mid-nineteenth century to turn the town into a major port serving Ireland and Scotland. He commissioned the famous architect Decimus Burton to plan the new town.

In order to improve navigation into the port, it was necessary to build three lighthouses to guide shipping through the treacherous Wyre estuary. The best known is perhaps the Upper Lighthouse, more popularly known as the Pharos (after the ancient lighthouse of Alexandria), which comprises a 93-foot-high sandstone column. The light is approximately 104 feet above sea level, and has a range of around 9 miles. Inside, there are 107 steps and a 10-foot ladder to get to the top. Unfortunately, it is not open to the public.

The Pharos or Upper Lighthouse, Fleetwood.

The Beach or Lower Lighthouse, Fleetwood.

The lighthouse was for a long time painted in a noticeable red and cream colour, which was removed in the late 1970s. The current terminus of the tramway to Blackpool adjoins the foot.

Fleetwood's second lighthouse is the Lower or Beach Lighthouse, opposite the North Euston Hotel. Only 34 feet high, this is built in a neoclassical style with a square colonnaded base having an octagonal gallery and lantern.

Both lighthouses first shone on 1 December 1840. They were designed by Decimus Burton in accordance with the navigation plan of Captain Henry Mangles Denham. By lining the two lights up, with that of the Pharos always being higher than the Beach lighthouse, safe passage for ships was assured.

A third lighthouse was also built. Known as the Wyre Light, it was built by the blind engineer, Alexander Mitchell, and is some 2 miles offshore at the northern end of North Wharf. It is believed to be the first lighthouse built using screw piles in the UK. It was provided as the starting point for ships lining themselves up by means of the other two lights, but has not been used for this purpose for some considerable time and is now derelict.

The Pharos and Beach lighthouses are both still in use, being controlled by the Port of Fleetwood. They are now lit by electricity.

Sir Peter's ambitions for Fleetwood were short-lived, as the rapid development of the railway system in early Victorian times; particularly the West Coast Main Line provided easier access to better ports. The street layout of the northern end of Fleetwood, and some of its architecture, particularly the North Euston Hotel and the lighthouses, provide reminders of these early plans.

*Access: On the Esplanade and Pharos Place at the northern end of the town. FY7 6BN.*

# Gems of Preston, Chorley, South Ribble and West Lancashire

## 43. Avenham and Miller Parks, Preston

The area around Avenham and Miller Parks forms a surprisingly pleasant part of Preston. Leading from Avenham Lane is Avenham or Ladies Walk, which predates the park. This was bought for £15 in the year 1697 and completed the year after. The two lower walks were added in the 1860s when the parks were being laid out after Joseph Livesey, a local philanthropist and social reformer formed a relief committee to provide unemployment relief due to the lack of imported cotton during the American Civil War.

The Belvedere, Avenham Park, Preston.

Sebastopol Cannon, Avenham Park, Preston.

Walking along Avenham Walk, on the right-hand side is the Belvedere. This now stands on the site of the winding house, demolished in 1869, of the old freight tramway to Walton Summit. It is a Grade II listed building and was first erected in the adjacent Miller Park in 1865 at a cost of £468, but was moved here in 1875 having made way for the Earl of Derby statue in that park.

Adjacent to the Lower Viewing Terrace, which leads to the steps to the lower part of the park, these two replica Russian cannon captured after the fall of Sebastopol in the Crimean War of 1854–55 can be found. They were placed here during the park's recent restoration.

The original cannon were 36 pounders presented to Preston in 1858. Two local regiments, the 30th and 47th, had taken part in the successful Siege of Sebastopol, the capture of which effectively ended the war.

Adjoining Avenham Park is Miller Park. The land for this was bought in 1863 by Thomas Miller, a local cotton mill owner. It was laid out to a design by Edward Milner with the aim of providing unemployment relief during the 'cotton famine' mentioned above.

The park is more formal than its neighbour. It includes a large statue of the 14th Earl of Derby, Prime Minister from 1866 to 1868. There is also a grotto, at the entrance to which are two small pieces of hexagonal basalt from the Giant's Causeway in Northern Ireland.

*Preston's Harris Museum and Art Gallery, located in a striking building in the city centre, is well worth a visit.*

*Access: Avenham Park is best approached from Avenham Lane, to the south of the city centre. PR1 8JP.*

Basalt Blocks from the Giant's Causeway, Miller Park, Preston.

# 44. Hoghton Tower and Samlesbury Hall

Hoghton Tower is one of Lancashire's stately homes and is well worth a visit. It has been the home of the Hoghton family since the twelfth century.

The current building was completed by Thomas Hoghton in 1565, and retains its fortified manor house character, being built on top of a hill. It is claimed as the only true baronial residence in Lancashire.

In 1617, Sir Richard Hoghton invited King James I to visit him on one of his journeys. The visit lasted only a few days, but the costs incurred bankrupted his host. A length of red velvet carpet covered the entire driveway, a considerable distance. Accommodation and barracks were built for the king's large retinue of troops and nobility.

The king was very security conscious and sought the safest bedroom in which to sleep to minimise the chances of being murdered. When he arrived on his horse, he continued straight through the door on the horse, up the stairs and along the passageway until he found a bedroom at the end with only one entrance, which could more easily be guarded.

While eating in the Banqueting Hall, the king was so impressed with a loin of beef that he took his sword and 'knighted' it 'Sir Loin', although this amusing story is not substantiated.

Hoghton Tower, exterior of the Banqueting Hall.

The Hoghtons fought for the Crown during the Civil War and the tower was besieged by Parliament. When it eventually fell, the Roundheads entered the powder magazine contained in the tower, which stood between the two courtyards. The magazine then exploded killing over a hundred people. This tower, which gave its name to the building, has never been rebuilt.

A period of neglect followed when the family moved away in the late eighteenth century, but restoration began in 1870 and was completed in 1901. Over the years, many notable people have visited or stayed in the tower, including King William III, King George V and Queen Mary, Prince Philip and the former US Secretary of State Condoleezza Rice. William Shakespeare is also thought to have stayed there as part of a group of travelling actors.

See also the Tudor Well House, which contains a well that is 120 feet deep. The horse-drawn winding gear can be seen in the courtyard.

\*

The delightful timber-framed building of Samlesbury Hall was built around 1325 by Gilbert de Southworth of Warrington. It is described as both 'Lancashire's historic home' and 'Lancashire's friendliest home'. The Southworths were one of Lancashire's great Catholic families, and naturally there is a priest hole. In one of the main rooms is an elaborate fireplace installed by Sir Thomas de Southworth in 1545.

In 1677–78 it passed to Thomas Bradyll, who stripped many of the interior fittings for reuse at Conishead Priory near Ulverston. It was then let to handloom weavers.

In 1830 it became a public house, the Bradyll Arms, and then in 1850 it became a Pestalozzian-style boarding school. Reverting to a private house by 1862 it was

*Above*: Main entrance of Hoghton Tower.

*Below*: Horse gin at Hoghton Tower.

*Above*: Samlesbury Hall on the day of a vintage motor rally.

*Below*: The elaborate Parlour fireplace installed by Sir Thomas Southworth in 1545.

occupied until around 1909.The year 1924 saw it being bought by contractors for demolition to build a housing estate in the grounds. After a public outcry, the Samlesbury Hall Trust was set up by six local businessmen to raise money to buy the hall, which occurred the following year.

The trust continues to run the hall. It is open most days, Saturdays excepted, and entry is free of charge. As well as the hall, there is a Victorian garden, woodland walks, a bee and heritage centre and other features.

*Access: On the northern side of the A675 between Blackburn and Preston. PR5 0SH. Samlesbury Hall is on Preston New Road, Samlesbury, PR5 0UP.*

# 45. Rivington Terraced Gardens, Tower and Sham Castle

The Bolton-born soap magnate William Hesketh Lever bought the Rivington Manor estate in 1900. After an unsuccessful legal battle with Liverpool Corporation over the Anglezarke reservoir scheme, he donated part of his purchase to Bolton Corporation. On 45 acres of the remainder he created the Rivington Terraced Gardens, originally called Roynton Gardens.

The Seven Arched Bridge, Rivington Terraced Gardens.

The Seven Arched Bridge with the loggia in the background.

The Japanese Lake.

In 1901, he built a large timber bungalow, Roynton Lodge. The gardens followed from 1905 to a design by the landscape architect Thomas Mawson, but Leverhulme kept close personal control. The scale of the project on such an inhospitable site was amazing, and yet elegant walks, lawns, terraces, a Japanese Garden (with lake, waterfalls, 'tea houses' and lanterns) and bridges were all laid out. A seven-arch bridge, said to have been designed by Leverhulme himself, was built in 1910–12. The Japanese Garden, on which work started in 1922, was said to have been inspired after Lever visited Japan.

At the top of the gardens is the three-storey Pigeon Tower, built in 1910. It contains Lady Lever's Sewing Room on the top floor while the lower floors housed doves and pigeons.

In 1913, the Roynton Lodge was burnt down by Suffragette Edith Rigby. Leverhulme replaced it with a larger stone bungalow. After his death in 1925, the gardens passed to the Bolton brewer John Magee, and in 1949 to Liverpool Corporation. By this time, after a period of neglect, the bungalow was demolished.

For many years, the gardens were abandoned, but since 1974 some restoration work has been carried out by the Conservation Volunteers aided by the site's owners, now United Utilities, who have leased the gardens to the Rivington Heritage Trust. A more substantial restoration scheme costing £4 million is under way at the time of writing (2018) after a grant from the Heritage Lottery Fund.

On top of Rivington Pike, at a height of 1184 feet above sea level, is a tower, which was built as a shelter and vantage point in 1733 by John Andrews after he inherited one half and bought the other half of the Rivington Manor estate in 1729. It is claimed to celebrate him gaining ownership of the full manor, but this was not

*Left*: The Pigeon Tower, Rivington Terraced Gardens.

*Below*: Rivington Pike Tower.

the case. The Shaw family had always retained a one-eighth share. The stone used was taken from the original beacon platform and from the bed of the River Douglas. It is a square tower and is 20 feet high.

At one time it had a wooden roof and windows in all sides. The single room on the ground floor measured 13 feet square with a stone flagged floor, a fireplace and a cellar. It was used for shelter when grouse shooting parties visited the moors, but this stopped when Lever bought the estate. The tower was restored in the 1990s and has long been bricked up. It is a Grade II* listed building. The walls contain many examples of graffiti, some from the last century.

The nearby village of Rivington is also worth a brief look. The Anglican church is unusual in that it is not dedicated to anyone and is simply known as 'Rivington Church'.

The Sham Castle looks like one of many typical ruined castles, built around a courtyard plan. It stands in a commanding position over Rivington Reservoir on a mound called Coblowe Hillock and has thick walls and typically castle-like features.

The truth is this castle was started in 1916 by Lord Leverhulme on some land retained by him. It is so convincing because it is an exact replica of Liverpool's *genuine* ruined castle, which was demolished in the 1720s to make way for easier traffic access to the city. It is said that Lever deliberately chose to build a replica of the former Liverpool Castle after he had lost his case against Liverpool Corporation over the construction of the Anglezarke reservoirs.

There were never more than a couple of workmen on the project and it was left unfinished on his death in 1925.

*Access: Via the car park (very busy at weekends) at Rivington Hall Barn. BL6 7SB.*

*For the castle, park at the main visitor centre at Great House and walk along the reservoir southwards for around ten minutes. BL6 7SB.*

Exterior view of Sham Castle, Rivington.

Interior view of Sham Castle, Rivington.

# 46. Scotsman's Stump, Winter Hill

On the opposite side of the roadway just beyond the television tower is this metal stump, complete with inscription, which was placed here in 1912

The stump commemorates a young Scotsman, George Henderson, who was brutally shot in the face and killed at noon on 9 November 1838.

Henderson originated from Annan and was working as a travelling salesman for a Mr Jardine, a Blackburn draper. He often walked over the moors between Bolton and Blackburn and on the fateful day was returning to Blackburn having visited a nearby inn.

There were a number of people on the moor that day, although it was shrouded in autumn mist. One of them, twenty-two-year-old James Whittle, had borrowed a gun, was charged with Henderson's murder and stood trial at Liverpool. However,

Scotsman's Stump, Winter Hill.

the main prosecution witness, James Halliwell, was not reliable, and could indeed have been the murderer. As a result, Whittle was acquitted. Today the murder remains unsolved.

The stump was erected after public subscription and replaced an earlier tree (some say a gatepost), which stood nearby.

*Access: The road to the television tower, operated by Arquiva, leads northwards off George's Lane, which leads northwards off Chorley Road (B6226). A small car park is a third of the way up, beyond which the road is private and can only be used as a footpath. A twenty-minute walk uphill leads towards the television tower. BL6 6XL.*

*While in the area, take the opportunity to visit Turton Tower, on the western side of Chapeltown Road (B6391) BL7 0HG.*

Plaque at Scotman's Stump.

# 47. Some Smaller Gems in Leyland and Chorley

Worden Park is a true asset to the town of Leyland and is very popular with the locals. It opened to the public in 1951, having originally been the seat of the Ffarington (sometimes spelt Farington) family.

Worden Hall, in the park's centre, had been partially destroyed by fire some ten years earlier, leaving only one wing now standing. The surrounding buildings house an arts centre, theatre and a craft centre. Elsewhere there are miniature railways and an ice house.

The maze dates to the mid-nineteenth century and was designed by William Andrews Nesfield, a renowned engineer and landscape designer. Nesfield had designed a similar maze at Somerlyton Hall in Suffolk.

It formed part of the formal gardens and is planted with hornbeam with a lime tree at its centre. It has two entrances, one being a false one that only leads to dead ends.

The maze is free of charge to enter.

The Hedge Maze at Worden Park, Leyland.

The British Commercial Vehicle Museum, Leyland.

While in Leyland, do take a look inside the British Commercial Vehicle Museum. Dating from 1983, this museum is located within the old Inspection Building of the original Leyland Motors factory. It contains a fascinating collection of commercial vehicles dating back to the 1800s, together with other vehicles such as buses, fire engines and the 'Popemobile' built in Leyland for the 1982 visit to England by Pope John Paul II. Special events are held from time to time and guided tours are available. At the time of writing the building was closed for a major revamp.

*

Simon Jenkins in his 2009 book *England's 1,000 Best Houses* describes Astley Hall as 'the most exhilarating house in Lancashire'. It is a superb Jacobean building, constructed around an Elizabethan courtyard, extended in 1630 and 1653 and finished around 1666 by Margaret Charnock and her husband Richard Brooke.

The interior is well worth a look, with impressive plasterwork ceilings showing wreaths and cherubs in both the Great Hall and the Drawing Room. There are also numerous inset paintings of important historical figures, including Christopher Columbus and Elizabeth 1. Covering the entire width of the top floor is a long gallery, a must-have asset of the time, which in turn contains a 23.5-foot-long shovelboard table, one of the finest in existence.

A south wing and the stuccoed exterior were added in 1825. Reginald Tatton gave the hall to Chorley Council in 1922 to honour local men killed in the First World War. The park has recently been substantially renovated with the aid of a grant from the Heritage Lottery Fund. Entry is free of charge.

Included in the nearby Coach House is the 'Chorley Remembers Experience', an exhibition and display space devoted to the town's military history over the years.

*Above*: Astley Hall, Chorley.

*Below*: Courtyard view, Astley Hall.

*Access: Via Worden Lane on the south side of Leyland. From the park's car park, go round the back of the main park buildings and the Maze is on the right hand side. PR25 1DJ.*

　*The British Commercial Vehicle Museum is located on King Street PR25 2LE. For Astley Hall use PR7 1XA.*

# 48. Ormskirk Parish Church

This church boasts both a steeple and a spire, one of only three churches in the UK to be so blessed, and the only one with both at the same end of the building.

Legend has it that the local Viking leader Orme, in the nineth century, provided it with both a tower and steeple to satisfy his two daughters (some say his sisters), one of whom wanted a tower and the other a steeple.

Although the church has Saxon origins, the tower legend is unlikely. The steeple dates from the early fifteenth century, although the original structure blew down in

Ormskirk Parish Church.

1731 and was rebuilt between 1790 and 1832. The tower was built in 1548 to house the bells of Burscough Priory following the Dissolution of the Monasteries. One of these bells remains in the church.

*Access: In the centre of the town on Church Street, L39 3AJ.*

# 49. Rufford Old Hall

The earliest recorded date of a hall in existence at Rufford is around 1450, the estate having been gradually built up by the Hesketh family since the mid-thirteenth century.

In the early sixteenth century, an illegitimate son, Robert Hesketh, inherited the estate, and built the present-day Great Hall. It clearly indicates not only the wealth and position of the family, but was also intended to establish Robert's place within it. The Great Hall has a splendid hammer beam roof and an intricately carved movable wooden screen, which some have claimed is the world's biggest draught excluder.

Rufford Old Hall.

Moveable wooden
screen in Rufford
Old Hall.

It is rumoured that the young William Shakespeare performed here from around 1581. Shakespeare had been employed by Alexander Hoghton of Lea Hall near Preston as a tutor, and in this role he would have been expected to entertain guests. In his will Hoghton gave instruments and costumes to Thomas Hesketh together with an instruction to 'look after his household'.

The hall was substantially extended in 1661 by a three-storey red-brick wing, and a third wing was added in 1820. The family seat later moved to the nearby Rufford New Hall and then to Northamptonshire in 1867. The Old Hall was given to the National Trust in 1936.

The hall is said to be haunted with several ghosts and has featured on the *Most Haunted* TV series.

*Access: On the western side of the A59, just north of Rufford village. L40 1SG.*

# 50. Parbold Bottle

This curious monument was built in 1832 to commemorate the Reform Act, which extended voting to the middle classes. This had been achieved despite strenuous Tory opposition, which had been overcome when additional peerages for supporters of the Act were created to get the legislation through the House of Lords. At the same time, the boundaries of parliamentary constituencies were considerably altered.

The 'bottle' is some 6.5 feet high, built from local gritstone and shaped like an antique bottle. It was destroyed by a gale in 1942, but subsequently restored.

Local legend claims that anyone who can leapfrog it will be blessed with four fingers, thumbs and the ability to walk upright – apparently some say that this is not normal in Parbold!

*Access: On the eastern side of Parbold, just off the A5209. Take the footpath that is next to the old tip entrance, down the hill from the layby. WN8 7TG.*

Parbold 'Bottle'.

# About the Author

Robert Nicholls has lived in the North West since 1973, holding various professional positions in local government and subsequently with Manchester Airports Group. Born in 1952 in Sheffield, he was educated at High Storrs Grammar School, has a degree in Estate Management from Reading University and is qualified as a chartered surveyor. In 2000, he gained an MBA from Lancaster University and in 2014 he was awarded, with distinction, the Advanced Diploma in Local History by Oxford University.

He retired in 2013, having served twenty-five years with the Manchester Airports Group, latterly as Regulation Manager.

He is interested in local and transport history with particular emphasis on related economic development and land use changes. His previous publications include *Manchester's Narrow Gauge Railways* (1985), *Looking Back at Belle Vue* (1989), *Heyhead Church 1862–1992* (1992), *The Belle Vue Story* (1992), *Trafford Park: the First 100 years* (1996), *Curiosities of Greater Manchester* (2004), *Haveley Hey School: Seventy Years of Service to the Community* (2005), *Curiosities of Merseyside* (2005), *The Church of the Ascension: A History 1970–2006* (2006), *St Chad's Church, Ladybarn: The Story of a Church and Its People* (2007), *Curiosities of Cheshire* (2010), *Davyhulme Sewage Works and Its Railway* (2015), *50 Gems of Staffordshire* (2017) *and Secret Stafford* (2018). Kindle publications have included *Staffordshire Curiosities, Curiosities of the High Peak* and *The Curious Places of Lancashire*.

As well as contributing articles to magazines, he gives talks to local history societies.